Made in the USA
Monee, IL
23 August 2021

76347018R00070